Introducing
1 & 2 Kings

Introducing
1 & 2 Kings

A Book for Today

BOB FYALL

Series Editor: Adrian Reynolds

PTRESOURCES

CHRISTIAN
FOCUS

Unless otherwise indicated all Scripture quotations are taken from the Holy Bible, New International Version. Copyright © 1973, 1978, 1984 by International Bible Society. Used by permission of Hodder & Stoughton Publishers, a member of the Hodder Headline Group. All rights reserved. 'NIV' is a registered trademark of International Bible Society. U.K. trademark number 1448790.

Copyright © Bob Fyall 2015

ISBN 978-1-78191-606-3

Published by
Christian Focus Publications,
Geanies House, Fearn,
Ross-shire, IV20 1TW, Scotland.
with
Proclamation Trust Resources,
Willcox House, 140-148 Borough High Street,
London, SE1 1LB, England, Great Britain.
www.proctrust.org.uk

www.christianfocus.com

Cover design by DUFI-art.com
Printed by Bell and Bain

CONTENTS

Editor's Preface

First and Second Kings (really one long book) contain some of the most well-known Old Testament stories (think of the Queen of Sheba or Elijah and Elisha) and yet remain some of the least known books of the Old Testament. How has this turn of events come about? In part, at least, it is because we tend to cherry-pick exciting stories and take them away from their Bible context.

There is nothing inherently wrong with that if we make every effort to understand the stories correctly, but the truth is that the best way to read a story well is to read it in its context – and for us that means reading it as part of a larger book.

These two Old Testament books are narratives. I prefer to call them Old Testament story – not in the sense that something is made up, but in the sense that most of us would understand: these are not history books, for example, or lists of facts and figures. Rather, they are wonderfully and expertly crafted accounts with pace and character and important dialogue.

Our doctrine of the Bible means that we know that these stories are divinely inspired. They are part of the 'breathing out' of Scripture that Paul describes to young Pastor Timothy (2 Tim. 3:16). However, the mechanism of inspiration is that human authors are carried along by the Spirit and thus we have more (though not less) than divine stories. We have accounts which stir the human emotions. We smile. We cry. We laugh. We get angry. We are amazed. It's impossible to read 1 & 2 Kings without feeling all of this and more.

What we need then is some basic help to read these books well. Each volume in this little *Introducing* series started life as a much longer book, in this case *Teaching 1 Kings*. Our Teaching series is written by preachers for preachers and teachers to help them proclaim the Scriptures faithfully. Each book takes readers carefully through the Bible material, pointing out the big themes and main topics as well as helping in how we should apply the Scriptures as Christians.

Teaching 1 Kings was written for us by Bob Fyall. Bob is an experienced preacher himself and a long-standing teacher of teachers. He is thus able to get right into the groove of 1 Kings and help Bible preachers and teachers wrestle with the things they need to get right. If you enjoy this little introduction and you have any Bible teaching role in the church, we heartily recommend the longer volume.

However, Bob is also a good pastor. He is able to connect the Bible text to Christ (as all preachers must) and do so engagingly and winsomely in a way that makes the stories come alive for twenty-first century Christians. He does this by getting the basics right – which is why this little introduction is so valuable. Here are Bob's basics on 1 & 2 Kings! You will – I'm sure – find them very helpful indeed.

Perhaps you're about to read 1 & 2 Kings in your devotions? Perhaps there's a series starting at church or in your small groups? Perhaps it's a part of the Bible you don't know that well? Whatever your circumstance, you will discover that this little introduction will stir your interest and help you to get to grips with the text – which is, after all, what we all want.

God has spoken, and God continues to speak in His Word. Our sincere prayer is that this little accompanying volume will help you hear His voice. For the book of the Kings is truly a book for today.

About The Proclamation Trust

The Proclamation Trust is a U.K.-based charity that serves churches by championing the cause of expository Bible preaching and teaching. Our aim is to equip and encourage faithful Bible preachers and teachers wherever they may be found, but particularly in the U.K. We do that through our training course (the P.T. Cornhill Training Course, based in London) and through conferences, online resources and books. Our *'Teaching...'* series is a key part of that work and there are currently fifteen volumes in the series, including *Teaching 1 Kings* by Bob Fyall.

Our conviction is that expository Bible ministry soaked in prayer is the lifeblood of the local church. Expository ministry is Bible teaching where the tone, structure and aim of the sermon or Bible study reflect the tone, structure and aim of the passage itself. We recognise that the Holy Spirit has spoken in the Scriptures and it is the Bible preacher or teacher's job to 'give God the microphone'.

Thus, we believe that, by the work of the Holy Spirit, where the Bible is faithfully taught God's voice is clearly heard. The call of every Bible teacher is therefore to cast himself fully upon God and, in the words of the Apostle Paul to young Pastor Timothy, to 'correctly handle the word of truth' (2 Tim. 2:15). Many resources, including our blog for preachers and teachers, are available from our website, www.proctrust.org.uk, where you can also read more about our work and ministry.

Adrian Reynolds

April 2015

Bob Fyall is Senior Tutor in Ministry for the Cornhill Training Course in Scotland. He was formerly Director of Rutherford House, Edinburgh, minister of a parish church in Scotland, and pastor of a large student church in Durham, where he also taught Old Testament at Cranmer Hall.

Adrian Reynolds is part of the leadership team of The Proclamation Trust. He also serves as Associate Minister at East London Tabernacle Baptist Church. Prior to working for the Trust he served as a Baptist pastor in Hampshire, before which he worked in business.

I

Why read
1 & 2 Kings?

This is a really important question. It would be easy to dodge it and say, in effect, it's good to read 1 & 2 Kings (or 'Kings' as I shall call these books) simply because they are there. That's a good enough reason. If we are committed to the whole Bible as the word of God, then we shall value Kings as we do other parts. But more specifically, what is there about the book that makes its own unique contribution to the canon and makes it profitable as we follow the Lord? Four reasons can be given to help us to unpack the riches of this book.

1. KINGS IS GOD'S STORY ABOUT GOD

One of the ways in which Old Testament story works is by presenting truth indirectly as well as directly. What I mean is that in the narrative, without specific comment, the author shows us the nature, activities and ways of God through the flow of the story itself. Thus the cluster of Elijah stories in chapters 17–19 of 1 Kings, apart from the specific attack on idolatry, show us important truths about God in the way the narrative progresses. Thus we learn that He cares about physical needs and can supply these in unexpected ways (ravens and a widow in 17:6, 14; an angel in 19:5-7). He answers not fanatical ravings and hype, but simple, heartfelt prayer (18:27-29; 36-7). He does not dump His faithful servants on the scrap heap but allows them to rest and then gives them new tasks to do (19:5-8; 15-18).

Also, God's care for ordinary, often nameless, people is powerfully brought out in a chapter such as 2 Kings 4. There, those who receive the Lord's blessing through Elisha are otherwise unknown. That is not, of course, confined to this chapter: the wise treatment of the prostitutes by Solomon (1 Kings 3:16-28); the lepers in 2 Kings 7:9; the concern of Hezekiah for the ordinary citizens as they hear the Assyrian boasts (2 Kings 18:36) show similar emphasis.

There is also the activity of God in the events of history. He raises up kings against Solomon (1 Kings 11:23); controls events (1 Kings 12:15); removes His people to exile when they rebel against Him (2 Kings 17:20-23; 23:27). He acts in judgment: death by fire (2 Kings 1:12). He acts in mercy as the One who hears and answers prayer (for Elijah in 1 Kings 18:36-38; for Hezekiah in 2 Kings 19:14-19). Many similar examples could be cited, but these will suffice to show how awesome and gracious is the God of Kings.

In today's world these are truths which need to be proclaimed over and over again. Too often in pursuit of trying to deal with felt needs, we strive for a superficial relevance rather than allowing these great truths about God to fill our hearts and stretch our minds. Often, we believe in a tame domesticated God whose main function is to make us feel comfortable and offer quick fixes to deep-rooted problems. We need a God who can handle the giant evils of the world to all who repent.

Kings will point us to God Himself at the heart of the story, which is vital in the building of God-centred people which will encourage faith in God's promises and obedience to God's word. Since this is narrative, these great truths about God are embodied in real people and situations and this brings us to our next reason for reading Kings.

2. KINGS TELLS US ABOUT THE KINGDOM OF GOD

When we pray 'your kingdom come, your will be done on earth as it is in heaven', we know that prayer will only ultimately be fulfilled when the King returns and ushers in the new heaven and the new earth. However, it is also a prayer for that kingdom to be anticipated in our lives, both communal and personal. We also know only too well that values which are not kingdom values often predominate. Here in Kings we have a visual aid of an earthly kingdom which points to the future. This is an important point: at various times this small earthly kingdom was a genuine anticipation of the kingdom of our God and His Christ.

Unsurprisingly, the clearest glimpses of the kingdom come from the early and middle years of Solomon when the nation was united. The unity of God's people remains an important Biblical truth (John 17:22). But there are other important glimpses of how, even on earth, the kingdom is anticipated. In 1 Kings 3:7-15, the kingdom is strongest when the king rules with God-given wisdom. None of us is Solomon, but those in pastoral oversight need wisdom and the mind of Christ through listening to Him in His Word, and by His Spirit applying that word both to themselves and then others. The story of the two prostitutes (3:16-28) show that such rule is marked by compassion and a shrewd understanding of human nature.

First Kings 4 also shows wise administration of the kingdom and the fulfilment of the prophecy to Abraham in Genesis 15:18 that the kingdom would stretch from the

Nile to the Euphrates. These territories had been conquered by David (see 2 Sam. 8). Further wisdom involves intellectual, imaginative and aesthetic pleasure in God's creation. These emphases give a rich and rounded picture of human life, partial here but fully realised in the new creation. Understanding such truths will help to avoid the super-spirituality which denies the good gifts God has given us in this present life and has an unattractive and disembodied view of the new creation.

The next few chapters (5–8) show the genuine worship of the kingdom in the loving care lavished on the building of the temple. This is not to be pressed into service to prop up an ailing fabric fund. This is ultimately about building living stones in the temple of God's people: God's people in the Old Testament were an anticipation of the new creation. The high water mark is 8:27-30 where Solomon worships the

Lord who is both enthroned in the highest heaven but condescends to come into time and space. As any serious Bible student will be able to tell you the key to biblical theology is God up there (Gen. 1) who comes down here (Gen. 2), pointing to the perfect union of the new heaven and earth (Rev. 21:1-4).

There are other glimpses of the kingdom later in the book, not least in the goodly fellowship of the prophets (I will come to this shortly). However, even in days of decline, good things happen. Asa of Judah removed idolatrous practices in face of strong family opposition (1 Kings 15:11-14) a policy followed by his son Jehoshaphat (1 Kings 22:43). Jehosheba hides the young Joash, thereby saving the Davidic line (2 Kings 11:1-3). Hezekiah gives a glimpse of the Davidic kingdom, including defying the Assyrian Goliath (2 Kings 18–19). Josiah makes a valiant effort to reinstate the word of God at the centre of national life (2 Kings 22-23).

The kingdom is under persistent attack and this is the other side of the same coin: there is much to learn about this from Kings. We do not have to choose between focusing on the big picture of the kingdom and the ethical imperatives of that kingdom. To preserve the sheep we have to fight the wolf; to live according to kingdom principles we have to fight the enemies of the kingdom.

So, as we read Kings we will need to see the negatives as well as the positives. At the heart of Kings is the warning expressed by John at the end of his first letter: 'Dear children, keep yourselves from idols' (1 John 5:21). This perpetual temptation to build a visible kingdom which ultimately we can manipulate is first disastrously seen in the great Solomon himself (1 Kings 11:1-8). The whole sorry story continues to exile because once Yahweh becomes simply another mini-god, the distinctive kingdom lifestyle disappears. As we read this we need to examine our own idolatries, not least our evangelical ones: the celebrity culture; the obsession with numbers; the excessive busyness and the like. Each of us is in different situations with different idolatries. We also need to deal with the idols in our own hearts and it is surely significant that Solomon's idolatry was traced to his heart (1 Kings 11:4, 9).

3. KINGS TELLS US ABOUT THE WORD OF GOD
The book is dominated by the centrality of the word of God which saves and judges. This is established by David's last words to Solomon (1 Kings 2:2-4) and continued in the prophetic ministries of the great and the unknown; it culminates in the great reforms of Josiah (2 Kings 22 & 23). One thing this does is help to create and sustain confidence in the word of

God to do its work. This is a word which 'will not return empty... but achieve the purpose for which I sent it' (Isa. 55:11). We see this over and over again in the narrative of Kings.

Preachers today are not prophets, but we have all been given the prophetic word which, as Peter says, is 'a light shining in a dark place' (2 Pet. 1:19). At significant crisis points, prophets are involved bringing the word of God into the situation: Nathan in the accession of Solomon (1 Kings 1:22); Ahijah announcing the divided kingdom (1 Kings 11:29-39; 14:1-18); Elijah to the house of Omri (1 Kings 17–2 Kings 1) and Isaiah to Hezekiah (2 Kings 19:20-34). That does not mean that we can look at the politics of today and give authoritative messages to prime ministers and presidents as if we had God-given authority to pronounce on government policies. Rather, the general

principles of a world-view flowing from
a God of justice and mercy are the
foundation of truly biblical living and
God-fearing community.

Throughout Kings, as today, the word
of God is more important than the mes-
senger who brings it and it is a word of
challenge in the present which shapes
the future. It is encouraging to see how
the word is not bound by time; a striking example of this is when the man of
God from Judah prophesies to Jeroboam
about how one day a Davidic king called
Josiah will cleanse the land from idolatry
(1 Kings 13:2-3).

4. KINGS POINTS TO CHRIST

Christians are often uneasy about how to
see appropriate lines to Christ, and one
reason for the neglect of much of the
Old Testament is that many find it hard
to see Christ in the text. Thus there may
be a sermon on Esther which could have

been preached in the synagogue followed by some lame statement like 'it's really all about Jesus'. At this point we, the hearers, may legitimately scratch our heads and think 'Did I miss something?'

Or we've all heard Old Testament sermons where the passage may simply be used as a springboard to jump into the New Testament. Thus a sermon, allegedly on Isaiah 53, is in effect a sermon on Acts 8. However, we need to remember that the apostles and other preachers in the early decades preached from the 'Scriptures' by which, like the risen Lord on the way to Emmaus (Luke 24:27), they meant what we call the Old Testament.

At first sight Kings does not seem to be the most promising book from which to see Christ in all His glory, but if we take seriously the points already made about the nature of God and the kingdom, quite a different picture begins to emerge. The starting point is the emphasis on David and the Davidic dynasty. Neither David himself, nor even the most deserving of his sons, truly ruled over a kingdom whose throne was established forever (see 2 Sam. 7:13). Yet, as already noticed, there are tantalising glimpses of that kingdom and while in the northern kingdom, four dynasties rise and fall, the house of David persists to the Exile and beyond. Even in human terms, five hundred years is a long time for a royal house to survive.

Thus, in spite of the failures of the human kings, the hope still burns that one day there will be a son of David who will embody the covenant and fulfil all its promises. This is already implied in the words of Ahijah to Jeroboam that David's descendants would be humbled but not forever (1 Kings 11:39). Even Exile did not break the line of promise. The Davidic king, Jehoiachin, in exile in Babylon is raised to the highest place at the king of Babylon's table (2 Kings 25:27-30). This points to the day when the King reigns on the holy hill of Zion.

The reigns of the better kings, as already noticed, point to the time when David's Greater Son will reign over the whole of creation. But on the other hand the reigns of the bad kings point to the need for the true king who will reign in righteousness and peace. Idolatry and apostasy brought nothing but misery, tyranny and endless wars, and showed starkly the need for a different kind of kingdom. The words of David to Solomon (1 Kings 2:2-4) not only emphasise the centrality of the words of Moses but the vital importance of a son of the Davidic line who would embody their truth.

Kings is a vital stage in the journey which is to lead to the announcement to Mary by Gabriel that the Saviour to be born was the One to whom 'the Lord God will

give the throne of his father David, and he
will reign over the house of Jacob for ever;
his kingdom will never end' (Luke 1:32-33).
The phrase 'house of Jacob' neatly sums up
the book of Kings, as that name reminds us
of all the waywardness and sinfulness of
the people as God's abundant grace trans-
forms Jacob into Israel.

Similarly, Jesus is the true Prophet to
whom all the prophetic figures in Kings
point. But He is also the true Word, not
simply the One who brings that word. It
was from the book of Kings that He spoke
in His first synagogue sermon, speaking
of the grace of God to Gentile widows
and lepers (Luke 4:24-27). And there He
was the object of hatred that is so often
the lot of the true prophet.

Seeing Christ in Kings is not an alien
construct imposed on the text but rises
naturally and inevitably from it. There are
different ways to do this, but we need to be

sensitive and not over-allegorise, for example making too much of all the details of the temple furnishings, but our task as faithful readers is to see the living Word as He appears in the pages of the written word: this is not so much having a checklist imposed on every passage as developing an ear to hear the Master's voice.

2

Finding your way around Kings

For many, tackling the books of Kings is like embarking on a rather unfamiliar sea with just a few well known islands, such as some of the stories of Elisha and Elijah. We reach these with relief and see the rest of the voyage as rather tedious and uninspiring. The brief notes on individual kings in passages such as 1 Kings 15 and 16 or 2 Kings 13–15, not to say the long details of temple building in 1 Kings 6 and 7, seem dull and lacking in either narrative drive or spiritual nourishment. Faced with this, many readers focus on the purple passages and neglect the rest of the books.

This is a great loss because the books are a unified and powerful story with a coherent message, and both strong narrative interest and relevant theology. There is a lot of hard work to be done but this will be wonderfully rewarding as we see God working His purpose out with flawed people, bringing His kingdom nearer, and pointing to the day when the true king will come. Our horizons will be expanded and our faith quickened as we look beyond our own little sphere and see God in the sweep of history. Our confidence in His Word will grow as we see that Word raise up and depose kings and empires; we will be able to read this as part of God's story about God, where the best of His servants only make it by grace and where human leadership depends on faithfulness to the Lord.

There are important issues of background to be covered as we approach these books, and we will need to look at such matters as place in the Bible, historical situation, genre and particular problems such as idolatry and judgment. Much of the terrain will be unfamiliar, but if we study diligently under the guidance of the Spirit we shall hear the Master's voice and see His face.

1. KINGS IN ITS SETTING
The place of Kings in the Bible
Kings is one book and the division is because of the amount of material which can usefully be included in one scroll. Its place in the Bible is first of all as a significant part of the Big Story which runs from creation to new creation and, more specifically along with 1 and 2 Samuel, a history

first of the united monarchy and then the divided kingdoms: the northern kingdom of Israel which fell to Assyria in 722 B.C., and the southern kingdom of Judah which was taken into exile in Babylon in 587 B.C. But the first hint of the story of the monarchy comes much earlier when God promises to Abraham (Gen. 17:6) and repeats to Jacob (Gen. 35:11) that kings will come from them. So this story is part of the promises to the patriarchs and points forward to the King who is to come (more of this later).

One other point to notice is that while we call Kings a history book (and it is not less than that), in the Hebrew Bible, the books of Joshua to 2 Kings (except for Ruth) are called 'the former prophets'. This is an important clue as to how we are to look at these books. This emphasis is seen in the large amount of space given to prophets, especially Elijah and Elisha, and the way history is seen as God unfolding His purpose.

Kings and history

One of the things which daunts readers is the length of the book. That, however, should not be exaggerated. The book of Kings in Eugene Peterson's *The Message*[1] runs to only 105 pages. That is not a lot in which to cover nearly 500 years. Imagine compressing the history of Britain from the reign of Elizabeth I to the reign of Elizabeth II into a book as short as that! So the first point to make is that the history is ruthlessly selective, and we shall see examples as we read our way through the book (for example, Omri, Ahab's father is dismissed in six verses, 1 Kings 16:23-28, although we know that he was a big player on the international stage and impressed the Assyrians). I've included a list of

1. Peterson, E, *The Message* (Carol Stream, U.S.: NavPress, 1993)

kings at the end of this short book for readers who want to see how everything fits together historically.

We also need to note that the book is no mere chronicle of events but a record of the living God active in history. This is important as we try to apply the book. We ourselves are not David (Solomon, Josiah, and so on) but we have David's God. What God writes large on the pages of history reveals the kind of God He is, and thus how He is to be worshipped and obeyed. What Paul says, speaking specifically of Numbers, 'these things occurred as examples to keep us from setting our hearts on evil things as they did' (1 Cor. 10:6) applies to the rest of the Old Testament. Indeed, since Paul goes on to speak particularly about idolatry, the relevance to Kings is obvious. Thus, while in Kings we are meeting people who actually lived and reading about events which actually happened, we are not taking an antiquarian interest in the book. We are seeing windows into God's purposes and learning how to live lives which honour Him in the present world as we wait for the kingdom. This is a book which will lead us to pray 'your kingdom come, your will be done on earth as it is in heaven'.

The book begins with David at the end of his life and continues with a glimpse of glory days under Solomon, but this glory fades rapidly before the end of his reign and the kingdom is soon split under his foolish son Rehoboam. The northern kingdom lapses entirely into idolatry and much of the southern kingdom's story is similar, punctuated by a number of relatively good kings such as Asa and Jehoshaphat and two notable Davidic kings, Hezekiah and Josiah, but exile in Babylon looms and Zion mourns. Both kings are talked about in terms which specifically recall David. Hezekiah 'did what was right in the eyes of the LORD just as David his father had done' (2 Kings 18:3). Josiah 'did what was right in the eyes of the LORD and walked in all the ways of his father David' (2 Kings 22:2).

So what is the book about? Can we find a theme which unites the disparate material and which helps us to set about teaching it?

2. THE THEME OF KINGS

Early in the book (1 Kings 2:2-4) we find, I believe, the key which will unlock the riches of the book.

> 'I am about to go the way of all the earth,' he said. 'So be strong, show yourself a man, and observe what the LORD your God requires: Walk in his ways, and keep his decrees and commands, his laws and requirements, as written in the Law of Moses, so that you may prosper in all you do and wherever you go, and that the LORD may keep his promise to me: "If

> your descendants watch how they live,
> and if they walk faithfully before me with
> all their heart and soul, you will never fail
> to have a man on the throne of Israel.'"

These are David's words to Solomon as David bows out. The supreme authority of the words of Moses, which are the words of God, is to be the charter of the kingdom for both king and subjects. We might suggest that the book's theme could be expressed as 'ruling justly and wisely depends on obeying God's Word and this is not only true of the kings but of the people; disobedience is deadly'. The people cannot lead but they can choose to follow or not follow the Word of God. Both Hezekiah and Josiah were faithful to the Word of God but their reformations were dismantled after their deaths and the whole nation reverted to paganism.

This emphasis is underlined throughout the book with the Word of God coming through many named and unnamed prophets. The great central section of the book (1 Kings 17–2 Kings 13) is dominated by the ministries of Elijah and Elisha. Jonah is mentioned in 2 Kings 14:25. Isaiah plays a prominent role in 2 Kings 18 and 19. The great reforms of Josiah are given new impetus by the discovery of the Book of the Law (2 Kings 22:8). The exile is attributed to disobeying the prophetic Word (2 Kings 24:3).

Unpacking this a bit more, we can see how the word of promise and rebuke binds the book together. The Word of God covers the whole of life, but there are particular ways in which this theme is specifically treated in Kings. Three issues in particular deserve to be mentioned.

The Davidic King
The bookends of Kings draw attention to both the vulnerability of David's house and the enduring promise which sustains

it. At the beginning of the book, David lies weak and decrepit, but with the help of Nathan and Bathsheba rallies and secures the succession of Solomon and speaks to him the words already noted (2:2-4) about the future of the kingdom depending on obedience. At the end of the book (2 Kings 25:27), the Davidic king Jehoiachin is raised from prison to sit in a seat of honour at the table of the Babylonian king. That may be a long way from the kings of the earth honouring the Son of David but it is a light in a dark place. Zion is down but not out.

Throughout the book there is constant reference to the promise to David: the covenant with David of 2 Samuel 7 and Psalm 89. The references are multiple: 1 Kings 11:32; 15:4; 2 Kings 8:19; 20:6 are examples. These, coupled with the frequent references to the city of David and the commendation of Hezekiah

(2 Kings 18:30) and Josiah (2 Kings 22:2) for walking in the ways of David, show Yahweh's continuing favour to David's house. Also they point to his Greater Son (a subject we will return to shortly).

The Prophetic Word
As already mentioned, the story is punctuated by frequent references to the prophetic word, both in judgment and salvation. It would be tedious simply to give a list of references and a couple of examples will suffice. Six chapters (1 Kings 17–22) are given to Ahab and the prophetic word to him from Elijah, Micaiah and an unnamed prophet. These are words of judgment on Ahab and his house for idolatry, but all through the section there is the call to repent. Indeed when Ahab partially responds after his murder of Naboth and the grabbing of his vineyard (1 Kings 21:28-29), Yahweh delays the judgment. In chapter 22:19-23, the false words of the court

prophets are attributed to a lying spirit, but it is the words of the true prophet Micaiah which show reality.

Another example of the power of the prophetic word to save the godly and overthrow kingdoms occurs in 2 Kings 19. The Assyrian spokesman has boasted of the power of Sennacherib. His words are defied by Isaiah, who retorts with the word of Yahweh (vv. 21-29) and the great Assyrian army is destroyed. Plainly the power of the Word is at the heart of the story.

God's providence and human responsibility
In the unfolding drama of Kings, the responsibility to respond to the Word is central. The Word cannot be broken but human beings are not puppets, as we have already seen in the case of Ahab. The preaching of judgment is in fact a sign of God's grace because it calls for repentance and faith. A clear example of this is 1 Kings 11:29-39, where the

prophet Ahijah speaks to Jeroboam, using an acted parable of tearing his cloak into twelve pieces and giving ten of these to Jeroboam to symbolise the ten northern tribes of whom he is shortly to become king. Two tribes remain to the royal house of Judah because of the promise to David. Ahijah promises Jeroboam an enduring royal house as well (v. 38) but that promise depends on Jeroboam's obedience. Jeroboam is hardly crowned when he shows his faithlessness (12:28ff) and judgment is announced (14:6-12).

This emphasis of the challenge of the prophetic word continues, and even good kings like Hezekiah are judged if they turn to expediency and dangerous alliances rather than follow the path of simple obedience (2 Kings 20:16-18). This pattern of God speaking and humans responsible for hearing and acting is part of the great value of the book.

3. THE STRUCTURE OF KINGS

Taking it as a unified work one possible approach would be to see six main sections with further subdivisions:

1. Solomon's glory and disgrace (1 Kings 1:1–11:43). Solomon is an ambiguous figure and we shall explore this in the commentary.

   a. David bows out and Solomon succeeds to the throne (1:1-2:46). Here we see human vulnerability and divine promise.

   b. Wisdom in wise government (3:1 –4:34). Solomon at his best gives us a glimpse of the kingdom to come.

   c. Building projects (5:1-9:9): temple, palace and cities. The high water mark comes at 8:27-30.

   d. National and international activities (9:10–10:29) including the memorable visit of the Queen of Sheba.

   e. Ending badly (11:1-43). Solomon displays the tragedy of a divided heart.

2. A dismal bunch of kings (1 Kings 12:1–16:34)
   a. Bad in both north and south (12:1–14:31). There is a lot of prophetic activity, especially in chapter 13.
   b. Decline in Israel; better things in Judah (15:1–16:20), especially seen in the reign of Asa.
   c. Worse still (16:21-34). The house of Omri leads Israel to new depths.

3. Bringing God's Word in dangerous times (1 Kings 17:1–2 Kings 13:21); the stories of Elijah and Elisha. There is more in this long central section than the ministry of the two prophets but they dominate this part of the book.
   a. Elijah and Yahweh's powerful protection (17:1-19:21). God protects Elijah and shows the power of His Word.
   b. Ahab confronted by the prophetic word (20:1-22:40). Ahab is given chance after chance.
   c. Elijah's continuing ministry and

his ascension to heaven and Elisha comes into prominence (2 Kings 1:1–2:25).

d. Elisha's words and actions (2 Kings 3:1-9:13). These are both on the political stage and in private.

e. More politics (2 Kings 9:14–13:13). Jehu destroys house of Ahab; Athaliah tries to destroy house of David; Joash half-heartedly repairs the temple.

f. Elisha dies but brings life (2 Kings 13:14-21).

4. More bad kings (2 Kings 13:22–17:40)

a. Little to choose between Israel and Judah (13:22–15:38). Israel continues its downward spiral – things are only slightly better in Judah.

b. Goodbye Israel (17:1-41). The northern kingdom is exiled to Assyria and we see why this happened.

5. Reformers and wreckers (18:1–23:30). We see the two best kings since David but also the worst.

a. David comes again (18-20). Hezekiah stands up to the Assyrian Goliath but succumbs to flattery - like David he is flawed but faithful.

b. Judah's Ahab (21:1-18). Manesseh is the worst of all the kings. His behaviour makes exile inevitable; a footnote (vv. 19-25) talks of his equally godless son, Amon.

c. The word of Yahweh honoured (22:1–23:30). Josiah's great reformation comes too late to save the nation and he loses his life in an unwise battle with the Pharaoh.

6. Zion down but not out (23:31–25:30). These are the last dismal days of Judah leading to inevitable exile – but there is a hint of hope for David's line (25:27-30).

A much simpler outline would be to see three main sections:

1. The glimpse of glory (1 Kings 1-11)

2. The divided kingdom (1 Kings 12–2 Kings 17)
3. The closing years of Judah (2 Kings 18–25)

The weakness yet divine protection of the Davidic house with which the book begins and ends give the guiding thread of promise and fulfilment. It is also important with narrative to read large enough chunks to get the flow of the story as a whole.

4. Kings and Chronicles

The place of Kings in the Big Story, beginning with the promise of kings to Abraham (Gen. 17:6) and Jacob (Gen. 35:11), has already been noted, as has the significance of David and his sons. The apparent eclipse of that promise at the Exile is gloriously transformed with the words of Gabriel announcing the birth of great David's Greater Son 'the Lord God will give him the throne of his father David, and he will reign over the house of Jacob forever' (Luke 1:33). Paul, in Romans 15:12, speaks of the Davidic King reigning over the nations as the Gentiles gather to Christ. In Revelation, the 'Lion of the tribe of Judah, the root of David' opens the scroll of history (5:5). In Revelation 22:16 he is the origin and also the offspring of David.

However, there is one book which invites specific comparison with Kings and that is Chronicles (like Kings, one book but divided for convenience into two scrolls). Both cover similar ground but with different emphases. Kings shows why the exile happened, whereas Chronicles is written to encourage the remnant who returned from exile to see themselves in direct continuity with Moses and David as the covenant people whom God would continue to bless.

Thus many of David and Solomon's failures are omitted in order to emphasise their positive achievements as the foundation of Israel's hopes. The Chronicler particularly emphasises the extensive role of David in planning and providing for the work of the Temple (1 Chron. 22–27) as well as the orderly transfer of power from David to Solomon (1 Chron. 28–29). Also, there is far more extensive coverage of many of the kings of Judah: e.g. Jehoshaphat, the weak man who nevertheless trusted God in a crisis (2 Chron. 20); Uzziah the strong man discredited because of his pride (2 Chron. 26); the religious reforms of Hezekiah (2 Chron. 30–31); the belated repentance of Manasseh which failed to avert the Exile (2 Chron. 33).

The books of Kings and Chronicles complement each other, but the theology of a God who saves and judges is common to both. The genealogies which open Chronicles are a reminder of God's care for all His people and their personal importance to Him. Likewise the glories of David and Solomon anticipate the greater glory of the King who is to come.

It is important when we are reading in Kings not to import too much material from Chronicles but to focus on the particular emphases of the author. Otherwise we shall end up by seeing the Scriptures as a mishmash which does not do justice to either book.

An example of this would be the treatment of Jehoshaphat. In 1 Kings 22 –2 Kings 3 he appears as an associate of Ahab and then Jehoram. His reforms are not ignored (1 Kings 22:41-50) but the author's emphasis is on his unwise cosying up to Ahab's house. Kings does not deny that he was a good man but shows how he failed to realise his potential. Chronicles, while recognising his weakness, contains more detailed treatment of his reforms and especially his faith (in 2 Chron. 20) when he is faced with a vast army. Each book is contributing to the total picture but we need to stick to the text in front of us.

5. WHO WROTE KINGS?

The book itself gives no hint about who wrote it; the evidence of unified themes and careful planning suggests a single author. It was long believed that this was Jeremiah, not just because of the identical endings of the books (2 Kings 25 and Jer. 52) but because of a similarity in outlook and theology, not least the extensive treatment of the word of Yahweh. Clearly it cannot have been earlier than about 560 B.C., given the reference to Jehoiachin at the end of the book.

Obviously the author used sources such as royal annals, temple records and stories passed down in prophetic circles. The important thing is that this book is part of Scripture and is profitable whosoever the human author may have been.

3

How do Old Testament stories work?

Kings is part of the great narrative of the Bible which begins with creation and culminates in the new creation and, as we read it, we need to consider how we can handle narrative effectively. This is worth some brief consideration before we get to the text itself. The first thing that needs to be said is that, if we believe that God gave us the Bible, then *how* He says something will be a vital part of *what* He says.

Thus we will not read a story as if it was a doctrinal passage. We will be primarily interested in how God's story about God embodies the Gospel.

So what are the characteristics of narrative and how can we avoid moralising platitudes which is a constant danger in reading this kind of Bible book? We must remember these are, in many cases, exciting and gripping stories, and we need to enjoy reading them as we would any other good story. Not all of Kings is narrative of that kind: however, we need to be absorbed in the flow of the story and the place of individual episodes in the great narrative.

O.T. narrative, like any other story, has a number of components which together create the text. It is not a case of simply isolating these elements so much as seeing how together they create the story as we have it.

Plot is the first major part of story: the sequence of events, including principles of selection and the silences of the text. For example in Kings, the author gives a brief summary of the sequence of kings in 1 Kings 15 and 16 concluding with Ahab and we expect he will be dismissed in a few verses like his predecessors. However, the account of his reign spans chapters 17–22 because it is to be the backdrop to the ministry of Elijah and others, and to underline the supreme importance of the prophetic word. Hezekiah's religious reforms are given one verse (2 Kings 18:4) because again the emphasis is on the prophetic word brought by Isaiah. As we read the individual stories we will also notice the structure of the narrative and how the author's emphases are shown within episodes as well as the wider balance in the book as a whole.

Characterisation is another important element in story. God is the main actor but the part played by humans matters, hence the frequent references to David. Sometimes these characters will be developed at some length, notably Solomon. If the interpretation of Solomon in this book is accepted then we have a more convincing human being than if we see him as virtually flawless from 1 Kings 2–10 and then suddenly and without warning falling from grace in chapter 11. However it is not just the big players but the 'little' people who are vital in God's purpose, for example the little girl who told Naaman's wife about Elisha in 2 Kings 5:3 and the unnamed prophet who anointed Jehu in 2 Kings 9:6. Very often dialogue develops characterisation as in 1 Kings 1 and 2 where Solomon emerges as king.

Setting is important and often draws attention to deeper elements in the story. Warning bells ring in 1 Kings 10 at the elaborate luxury and extravagance of

Solomon's court (compare a similar technique in Esther 1 regarding the Persian court). Also the significance of Mount Carmel in 1 Kings 18 which emphasises that this contest of Yahweh and Baal is happening on Baal's home ground; if he cannot win here he cannot win anywhere.

Application needs to be considered carefully. Narrative is not normative: for example, 'David did well, so imitate him'; 'David did badly, so don't imitate him'. However, in a legitimate desire to avoid this kind of moralising, there has developed a tendency to flatten out every narrative in terms of the big picture. This results in very shallow understanding of these kinds of Bible books where virtually the same thing is understood in every passage. Also, a commendable desire to avoid moralising has led to a neglecting of the 'so what?' There are implications for our lives and Paul sets this out clearly in 1 Corinthians 10:1ff. These will follow from close understanding of the text and showing not only the big picture but showing how particular passages bring their own contribution to it.

Above all, we are not following a formula, we are developing an instinct for seeing each part of the Bible and each genre making their own unique contributions to the developing story. Kings speaks of a vital time in the history of God's people when they declined from the glory days of David and Solomon to bitter exile. Along the route prophets warned them, some good kings tried to stop the rot, but the dream ended in apparent failure. Yet, as we shall see at the end of the book in 2 Kings 25:27-30, there is hope beyond despair. We are part of that story and so the story speaks to us.

4

The kingdom
in danger
(1 Kings 1)

Some U.K. readers may recall the television programme 'After they were famous' which tells the story of people who briefly were stars of stage, screen or sports. Many simply returned to ordinary life, but there were also sad stories of early promise snuffed out by addictions and character flaws. As the book of 1 Kings opens, we have the melancholy feeling that here is David 'After he was famous'. The mighty warrior and great lover lies helpless in bed and the beautiful Abishag completely fails to arouse any response in him.

It seems all over, and God's promises to David seem to have become empty words at the mercy of political manoeuvring. We feel a sense of panic as the kingdom is in peril and, far from being the head of a dynasty (as Nathan the prophet had promised back in 2 Sam. 7:1-17), he looks like a tired old man in charge of nothing. So as we start reading the chapter we fear that God's kingdom has run into the sand.

CONTEXT AND STRUCTURE

The books of Kings form part of a much larger narrative and have an important place in the great story itself which runs from creation to new creation. More particularly it flows from the promise to Abraham that kings would come from his line (Gen. 17:16 and repeated to Jacob in

35:11). In the immediate context the story continues from 1 and 2 Samuel with the closing days of David and the rise of Solomon. The books cover more than 400 years from Solomon through to the divided kingdom and eventual exile of the northern kingdom to Assyria and the southern to Babylon.

The bulk of this long chapter deals with intrigues which are to result in the emergence of Solomon. We shall divide it into sections, following the flow of the narrative:

- The end of an era (1:1-4)

- Is David outwitted? (1:5-10)

- David's friends strike back (1:11-27)

- Don't underestimate David (1:28-40)

- Long live King Solomon (1:41-53)

Notice two general points: the first is that much of the story is advanced by dialogue which gives insight into the leading characters. The second is the idea of 'ruling' or 'sitting on the throne' (1:13, 17, 20, 24, 27, 30, 35, 46, 48). This is to be about who is reigning and whether, behind all human manoeuvring, The LORD is in control.

WORKING THROUGH THE TEXT
The end of an era (1:1-4)

This is the end of the story which began long before in 1 Samuel 16 when the young David was anointed and had eventually come to the throne. This chapter is one of the transition points where the leadership is about to be passed on. A good parallel is Joshua 23:1 where Joshua is also described as 'old and well advanced in years', and his death was shortly followed by apostasy and rebellion. This is a situation God's people often find themselves in: a leader influential in many churches and many lives passes away; a minister who has led wisely and well dies; a mentor is no longer there. What will happen now? In such circumstances we need to recall the words of Jacob to his sons: 'I am about to die, but God will be with you' (Gen. 48:21). God is in control; as John Wesley said, 'God buries his workers, and carries on his work'.

Yet the emphasis on the helplessness of David and the lack of his old vigour and shrewdness casts a deep unease over the chapter and a real fear for what is to happen. This is a crisis and a wrong move could mean disaster, not least the apparent failure of God's purposes. We are going to have to get used to that as we work through 1 and 2 Kings. This is not just the history of the kingdom of God then, it is the experience of that kingdom now.

Is David outwitted? (1:5-10)

At first sight it does indeed seem that the kingdom is in real danger of bad leadership, with the emergence of Adonijah who seizes the chance and 'puts himself forward'. This suggests a lust for power rather than a desire to serve, emphasised by his statement 'I will be king'. Here we have someone who is big on posturing and has an ego the size of a planet. It is important to see what the author is doing here. This is not a simple description of Adonijah's activities; rather he is giving us hints as to how to read the story.

True, he has a good conceit of himself and a big mouth, but there is more than that. The mention of Adonijah's handsome appearance recalls that of Absalom (2 Sam. 14:25-27), and earlier, Eliab (1 Sam. 16:6-7) and Saul (1 Sam. 9:2; 10:23-24). All these men, royal or potentially so, had looked impressive but had been rejected. The author wants to set Adonijah in that same line. There is also the problem that David had been too doting a father to him, as he had been to Absalom (compare v. 6 with 2 Sam. 14:1).

Who can say this is a merely ancient problem, a wholly unsuitable man setting himself in a place of leadership to which he has not been called and for which he is not qualified?

However, also like Absalom, Adonijah is not just a handsome playboy, but shows skill in building up support. He enlists the support of the wily Joab, commander of the army, someone whose ambiguous relationship with David is a recurring motif in 2 Samuel. Sadly, Abiathar the priest, who had been a crucial support for David at many points (1 Sam. 22:20-23; 23:9; 30:7), also joins the conspiracy. Adonijah cements this conspiracy by offering sacrifices at Enrogel, just south of Jerusalem; the pieties must be observed! Then a party is underway and the conspirators are riding high.

Adonijah is alive and well today. We meet him in the New Testament in 3 John 9-10 where he is called Diotrephes 'who loves to be the first', and who treats the church as his own private fiefdom where he can bully and lord it over God's people. We meet him in the church leader who cannot tell the difference between godly authority and bullying domination. We meet him in powerful cliques who try to push their own agenda and make life impossible for godly leaders. We meet him in our own hearts when the desire to be prominent at all costs is continually looking for an outlet.

David's friends strike back (1:11-27)
Adonijah, however, has overreached himself. One of those he failed to invite to his party was Nathan, and it is on Nathan that the spotlight now falls. The narrative here is gripping and exciting and makes much of its impact by direct speech. Repetition is cleverly used: verses 18 and 25 showing how advanced and formidable Adonijah's preparations are; verses 19 and 26 under-

lining who has been excluded, especially Solomon. Nathan goes first to Bathsheba (1:11-14) and reminds her of David's oath that Solomon would be king, and how this explains Adonijah's exclusion of Solomon from the feast (vv. 10, 19, 26). The stakes are raised as Nathan and Bathsheba both infer that once Adonijah reigned, Solomon and probably themselves would be eliminated (vv. 12, 21).

Bathsheba then reminds David of his responsibilities. He may be old and decrepit but 'the eyes of all Israel' (v. 20) are looking to him and expecting a statement on the succession. This is followed by Nathan himself visiting David and by actions (bowing) as well as words reminding him he is still king and has the power if he is willing to exercise it.

Three particular features of the story invite comment. The first is the circumstantial detail and the dialogue which draws us into the world of the story and helps us to see the characters as real flesh-and-blood people. These are real people facing a situation of tension and peril and not certain if they are going to succeed or even survive. This is what the life of faith looks like so often and one of the important themes in the historical narratives is to show how God's people often operate in a world where He appears to be absent. The most striking example of this is the book of Esther but we shall find many such passages in Kings (as there are in Samuel as well).

Second is the emphasis on human activity and decision-making. The account of David's last days in 1 Chronicles 28 and 29 emphasises God's overruling and is silent about these intrigues and conspiracies. These accounts are not contradictory but complementary. Chronicles underlines God's providence and the very

secondary nature of human involvement.
Here our author emphasises the very human and imperfect nature of the people
through whom these purposes are to be
fulfilled. Both these emphases are at the
heart of the life of faith. If we do not have
a firm belief in God's providence we will
quickly become discouraged. If we do not
have a realistic view of human nature, including our own, we will soon become dis-
illusioned.

Third is the key role of Nathan. This is
not the first time his intervention has been
crucial. After the dark story of David's
adultery with Bathsheba and murder by
proxy of Uriah (2 Sam. 11) which could
easily have ended the story, the words of
2 Samuel 12:1 – 'The LORD sent Nathan to
David' open the way for repentance and
grace. Here again, although no explicit
mention is made of the LORD sending him,
Nathan exercises a crucial service for the

kingdom. We are not Nathan, but we have Nathan's God and we need to be alert for opportunities, however small, to advance that kingdom.

Don't underestimate David (1:28-40)
We are quickly disabused here of any idea that David is 'past it' as, with his old vigour, he acts decisively and immediately sets in motion the process of Solomon's accession to the throne. Technically what happens here is that he appoints Solomon as co-regent with the promise that he will succeed him on the throne. This is underlined in the most binding way by linking it with his own experience of God's deliverance. And so, for the first time in this chapter, specific mention is made of how the Lord has been at work in this story which so far seemed only to be about human activity. The promise of 2 Samuel 7:12-16 about David's heirs will be fulfilled after all because God is on the

throne. It is this kingdom which will come and last forever.

Once again the true David is revealed, the one who was fully devoted to the LORD his God (11:4). He cared passionately for God's honour and that roused him from somnolence; we glimpse briefly the young man who defended that honour in the Valley of Elah so long before. This is his first concern and we cannot write him off as a spent force (1 Sam. 17).

Yet this is not simply a pious hope because words are followed by vigorous action. David calls Zadok and Nathan, representing the priests and prophets who have so much helped him both in his rise to power and his reign. They are joined by Benaiah the captain of his guard, who has also been sidelined by Adonijah, as public support begins to rally behind Solomon. The words 'Long live King Solomon' are the public declaration of the new regime and again the LORD's blessing is called on (1:36-37).

The loyalty of the army has been ensured by Benaiah, and the presence of the Kerethites and Pelethites (v. 38), mentioned in 2 Samuel 8:18 as part of David's bodyguard, has underlined this. The anointing of Solomon (v. 39) by Zadok recalls that of his father by Samuel (1 Sam. 16); 'All the people' (v. 39) probably is a contrast to the select group of followers clustering around Adonijah.

As we look beyond this to the bigger picture we should not ignore the detail in verse 37 – 'make his throne even greater than the throne of my Lord King David'. To some extent this did happen – see chapters 3 and following – but it is ultimately to be fulfilled in 'Great David's greater Son'. As we read Luke 1:32 ('The Lord God will give him the throne of his father David') we see this being fulfilled beyond

our wildest dreams. But just as Nathan
played a vital role earlier, so here the role
of the rejuvenated David is vital and must
contribute to the final assessment of this
truly remarkable man.

Long live King Solomon (41-53)
Adonijah's conspiracy collapses as suddenly as it began. Jonathan, Abiathar's son
(not the more famous Jonathan, David's
friend in 1 Samuel), must have witnessed
Solomon's coronation. He gives the main
point first: 'Our Lord King David has
made Solomon King' (v. 43). Just to underline this he describes those who have
now come out publicly for Solomon and
the popular support they have received.
Those around Adonijah see quickly the
way the wind is blowing and make themselves scarce (v. 49). Adonijah himself
flees for sanctuary and grasps the horns
of the altar; Solomon strikes a bargain
with him which falls short of a total am-

nesty shown by the absence of the words 'in peace' at the end of verse 53. It is hard to believe (and chapter 2 will demonstrate this) that Adonijah's 'loyalty' was more than skin deep: further problems lie ahead.

Applying the passage

Here are some ideas for how this passage applies to us as Christians today. Perhaps nowhere more than in Biblical story do we need to be sensitive and careful in our application. We will go wildly astray if we try the moralising approach: e.g. We need to be careful we don't become cold and apathetic like David but we need to have renewed spiritual energy (also like David); we must not arrange parties like Adonijah when we ought to be getting on with our business. Like all platitudes, these comments contain truths, but truths that have become soporific rather than life-changing and led essentially to a 'good works' gospel which is no gospel at all. We are not David, Solomon, Hezekiah, Josiah; but we have the same God as they did and that needs to be our starting point.

- The Bible is God's story about God and therefore we need to ask first what this chapter is saying about Him. We must see first of all His guiding hand behind these very political and 'unspiritual' events. God is in charge of His kingdom even when events conspire against Him. The kingdom, at this point of transition, looks very fragile and that is a stark reminder of how only the LORD can keep that kingdom safe and make it prosper.

- The other side of that coin is that even the best of God's servants only make it by grace. There is a constant temptation to exaggerate our importance in the kingdom and imagine our own right hand has saved us. Our evangelical celebrity culture aided by the internet has hugely overplayed our 'successes'. We need to be careful what we put on our church websites and other publicity material. The truth is that none of our churches, this side of glory, are all that impressive. Realising this will help us to avoid two pitfalls: one is despair as we feel our efforts are so futile; the other is conceit as we imagine our exploits are so magnificent. Rather we need to rejoice in the grace that saved us, wrote our names in heaven and now allows us to play our little part.

- We also see here the need for the life of faith to be lived in the messiness of human circumstances. The overruling hand of God does not mean that we 'let go and let God' but that we need to make choices, do what is right, and not simply become puppets.

- Here we have – as in all of 1 Samuel through to the end of 2 Kings – studies of leadership where we are given glimpses of both effective and ineffective kinds of rule. Adonijah is the self-promoting, self-appointed leader who imagines that the qualification for leadership is simply to say 'I am a leader'. We have the spiritual leadership of Nathan which is vital in the crisis. We have David who, all through his story, has shown a remarkable ability to 'come back' and a remarkable sense of God's deliverance which had kept him throughout his turbulent and eventful life.

- We must see this fragment of story as part of the Big Story. Indeed

1 and 2 Kings show their incom-
pleteness by beginning with the
close of David's reign and ending
with the Exile already many years
old. This is part of the same story
of faith as Abraham, particularly
that part in Genesis 17:6 where, to
promises of descendants and land,
God had added; 'I will make nations of you and kings shall come
from you'.

* The place of faith is vitally important, but even more so is God's faithfulness. A working title for a series
on Kings could be 'Faithful God,
Fickle People'. This is part of the
covenant (more in later chapters) by
which God pledges Himself to His
people, yet for that covenant to be
effective in our lives there needs to
be a loving response.

- Above all we need to find Christ in the text because the kingdom of David and sons is to be an acted parable on earth of the kingdom of his greater Son. That kingdom now often looks feeble and threatened; yet it will one day fill the earth.

Many of these points will come up again and again as you read through Kings.

LIST OF KINGS OF ISRAEL
(Dates of reigns are B.C. and all approximate)

THE UNITED KINGDOM		
Saul	1050-1010	-
David	1010-970	1 Kings 1:1
Solomon	970-930	1 Kings 1:30

THE DIVIDED KINGDOM					
Kings of Judah			Kings of Israel		
Rehoboam	930-913	1 Kings 11:43	Jeroboam I	930-910	1 Kings 11:31
Abijah	913-911	1 Kings 14:31	Nadab	910-909	1 Kings 14:20
Asa	911-870	1 Kings 15:8	Baasha	909-886	1 Kings 15:16
Jehoshaphat	870-848	1 Kings 15:24	Elah	886-885	1 Kings 16:8
J[eh]oram	848-841	2 Kings 8:16	Zimri	885	1 Kings 16:15
Ahaziah	841	2 Kings 8:25	Omri	885-874	1 Kings 16:16
Qu. Athaliah	841-835	2 Kings 8:26	Ahab	874-853	1 Kings 16:29
J[eh]oash	835-796	2 Kings 11:2	Ahaziah	853-852	1 Kings 22:40
Amaziah	796-767	2 Kings 14:1	J[eh]oram	852-841	2 Kings 1:17
Azariah	767-740	2 Kings 14:21	Jehu	841-814	2 Kings 9:1
Jotham	740-732	2 Kings 15:5	Jehoahaz	814-798	2 Kings 10:35
Ahaz	732-716	2 Kings 15:38	Jehoash	798-782	2 Kings 13:10
Hezekiah	716-687	2 Kings 16:20	Jeroboam II	782-753	2 Kings 14:23
Manasseh	687-642	2 Kings 21:1	Zechariah	753-752	2 Kings 14:29
Amon	642-640	2 Kings 21:19	Shallum	752	2 Kings 15:10
Josiah	640-608	2 Kings 22:1	Menahem	752-742	2 Kings 15:14
Jehoahaz	608	2 Kings 23:30	Pekahiah	742-740	2 Kings 15:23
Jehoiakim	608-597	2 Kings 23:34	Pekah	740-732	2 Kings 15:25
Jehoiachin	597	2 Kings 24:6	Hoshea	732-722	2 Kings 15:30
Zedekiah	597-586	2 Kings 24:17	*Fall of Samaria 722 B.C.*		

Fall of Jerusalem 586 B.C.

Introducing Series – New Testament

Introducing Acts (DAVID COOK)

Introducing Romans (CHRISTOPHER ASH)

Introducing Ephesians (SIMON AUSTEN)

Introducing 1 & 2 Thessalonians (ANGUS MACLEAY)

Introducing 1 Timothy (ANGUS MACLEAY)

Introducing 2 Timothy (JONATHAN GRIFFITHS)

978-1-84550-824-1

978-1-78191-233-1

978-1-78191-059-7

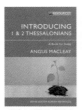

978-1-78191-326-0

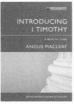

978-1-78191-060-3

978-1-78191-402-1

These are books which will equip you for ultimately teaching them. These are Pocket Guide versions of *Teaching 1 & 2 Thessalonians* (ISBN 978-1-78191-325-3), *Teaching 1 Timothy* (ISBN 978-1-84550-808-1), *Teaching 2 Timothy* (ISBN 978-1-78191-389-5), *Teaching Acts* (ISBN 978-1-84550-255-3), *Teaching Ephesians* (ISBN 978-1-84550-684-1), *Teaching Numbers* (ISBN 978-1-78191-156-3), *Teaching Romans vol. 1* (ISBN 978-1-84550-455-7) and *Teaching Romans vol. 2* (ISBN 978-1-84550-456-4). Each includes an introductory study.

Christopher Ash is Director of the Cornhill Training Course, a one-year course designed to provide Bible-handling and practical ministry skills to those exploring their future role in Christian work, and an active member of Christ Church Mayfair in central London.

Simon Austen has degrees in Science and Theology. A previous chaplain of Stowe School in Buckinghamshire, he is now Vicar of Houghton and Kingmoor in Carlisle, England.

David Cook has recently retired from his role as Principal and Director of the School of Preaching at Sydney Missionary and Bible College (SMBC). He is now involved in an itinerant preaching and teaching ministry.

Jonathan Griffiths serves as tutor on the Cornhill Training Course. He previously served as assistant minister at Christ Church, Westbourne.

Angus MacLeay is the Rector of St Nicholas, a large Anglican church in Sevenoaks, Kent, and is also a member of the Church of England General Synod.

Introducing Series – Old Testament

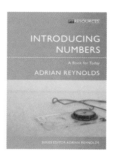

Introducing Numbers (ADRIAN REYNOLDS)
ISBN: 978-1-78191-158-7

Introducing 1 & 2 Kings (BOB FYALL)
ISBN: 978-1-78191-606-3

These are books which will equip you for ultimately teaching them. These are Pocket Guide versions of *Teaching Numbers* (ISBN 978-1-78191-156-3), *Teaching 1 Kings* (ISBN 978-1-78191-605-6). Each includes an introductory study.

Adrian Reynolds is Director of Ministry of The Proclamation Trust and also serves as associate minister at East London Tabernacle Baptist Church.

Bob Fyall is Senior Tutor in Ministry for the Cornhill Training Course (Scotland). Prior to that he was the Director of Rutherford House, Edinburgh. He is an experienced pastor, preacher and Old Testament scholar.

PT Resources

www.proctrust.org.uk
resources for preachers and Bible teachers

PT Resources, a ministry of The Proclamation Trust, provides a range of multimedia resources for preachers and Bible teachers.

Teach the Bible Series (Christian Focus & PT Resources)
The Teaching the Bible Series, published jointly with Christian Focus Publications, is written by preachers, for preachers, and is specifically geared to the purpose of God's Word – its proclamation as living truth. Books in the series aim to help the reader move beyond simply understanding a text to communicating and applying it.

Current titles include: *Teaching Numbers, Teaching Isaiah, Teaching Amos, Teaching Matthew, Teaching John, Teaching Acts, Teaching Romans, Teaching Ephesians, Teaching 1 and 2 Thessalonians, Teaching 1 Timothy, Teaching 2 Timothy, Teaching 1 Peter, Teaching the Christian Hope.*

Practical Preacher series
PT Resources publish a number of books addressing practical issues for preachers. These include *The Priority of Preaching*, *Bible Delight*, *Hearing the Spirit*, *The Ministry Medical*, *Burning Hearts* and *Spirit of Truth*.

Online resources
We publish a large number of audio resources online, all of which are free to download. These are searchable through our website by speaker, date, topic and Bible book. The resources include:

- sermon series; examples of great preaching which not only demonstrate faithful principles, but which will refresh and encourage the heart of the preacher

- instructions; audio which helps the teacher or preacher understand, open up and teach individual books of the Bible by getting to grips with their central message and purpose

- conference recordings; audio from all our conferences including the annual Evangelical Ministry Assembly. These talks discuss ministry and preaching issues.

An increasing number of resources are also available in video download form.

Online DVD
PT Resources have recently published online our collection of instructional videos by David Jackman. This material has been taught over the past 20 years on our PT Cornhill training course and around the world. It gives step-by-step instructions on handling each genre of biblical literature. There is also an online workbook. The videos are suitable for preachers and

those teaching the Bible in a variety of different contexts. Access to all the videos is free of charge.

The Proclaimer
Visit the Proclaimer blog for regular updates on matters to do with preaching. This is a short, punchy blog refreshed daily, which is written by preachers and for preachers. It can be accessed via the PT website or through www. theproclaimer. org.uk.

Christian Focus Publications

Our mission statement –

STAYING FAITHFUL
In dependence upon God we seek to impact the world through
literature faithful to His infallible Word, the Bible. Our aim is to
ensure that the Lord Jesus Christ is presented as the only hope
to obtain forgiveness of sin, live a useful life and look forward
to heaven with Him.

Our books are published in four imprints:

CHRISTIAN
FOCUS

popular works including biographies, commentaries, basic
doctrine and Christian living.

CHRISTIAN
HERITAGE

books representing some of
the best material from the
rich heritage of the church.

MENTOR

books written at a level
suitable for Bible College
and seminary students,
pastors, and other serious
readers. The imprint includes
commentaries, doctrinal
studies, examination of
current issues and church
history.

CF4•K

children's books for quality
Bible teaching and for all
age groups: Sunday school
curriculum, puzzle and activity
books; personal and family
devotional titles, biographies
and inspirational stories –
Because you are never too
young to know Jesus!

Christian Focus Publications Ltd,
Geanies House, Fearn, Ross-shire,
IV20 1TW, Scotland, United Kingdom.
www.christianfocus.com